...for Shadow and Sasha.

First Edition

Hardcover ISBN: 9798350950434
Paperback ISBN: 9781736574874
eBook ISBN: 9798350950441

Peculiar People and the Pets Who Love Them

by Justin Moroyan

Rosette and her poodle dress fancy each night.
Together, they stand by the street corner light.
Like clockwork, they remain for precisely 1 hour,
turning up their noses at all who alight.

You see, they have conditions exceedingly rare;
their senses of smell are reversed and quite strong.
In fact, the only smell they can stand to inhale,
is the 3 a.m. sewage the tide brings along.

It's pungent, compelling, and it's truly delightful.
It's blissfully inhaled 'til it finally lies...
deep in their nostrils where it provides a reprieve,
from that insufferable bakery across their street baking pies.

Quark, a deaf clown, invented some nicketts.
They fly in a swarm and sound awfully like crickets.

He'd hoped they'd infect the townsfolk with gladness...
but the constant chirping simply drove them to madness.

Ramses and his camel, Garak, left in search of a magical orb.
Reputedly, it turns sand to fruit punch.

One month in, they had some bad fortune...
a giant snake ate all their rations for lunch.

It's been 2 weeks since either has eaten.
Their lips have become all crackled and pasty.

Once in a while, they stare at each other.
They're both beginning to look mighty tasty.

Nanouk and his penguin fish every day.
The fish almost always wriggle away.

They're terrible fishers, unlike their mothers...
unlike their fathers, and unlike their brothers.

Princess Idle lived a life of great privilege.
She always got whatever she asked for.
She demanded a sloth, so the king got her one.
As always, she told him, "I'll want nothing more."

She and her sloth spent most their time dreaming.
Slow movement was also a trait that they shared.
Sometimes, so still, they were mistaken for corpses.
Checking her life signs, though, nobody dared.

She had a quick temper towards those who awoke her.
It was said that she fed the vines with her dreams.
Her exhausted servants did everything for her.
At being lazy, she and her sloth were a team.

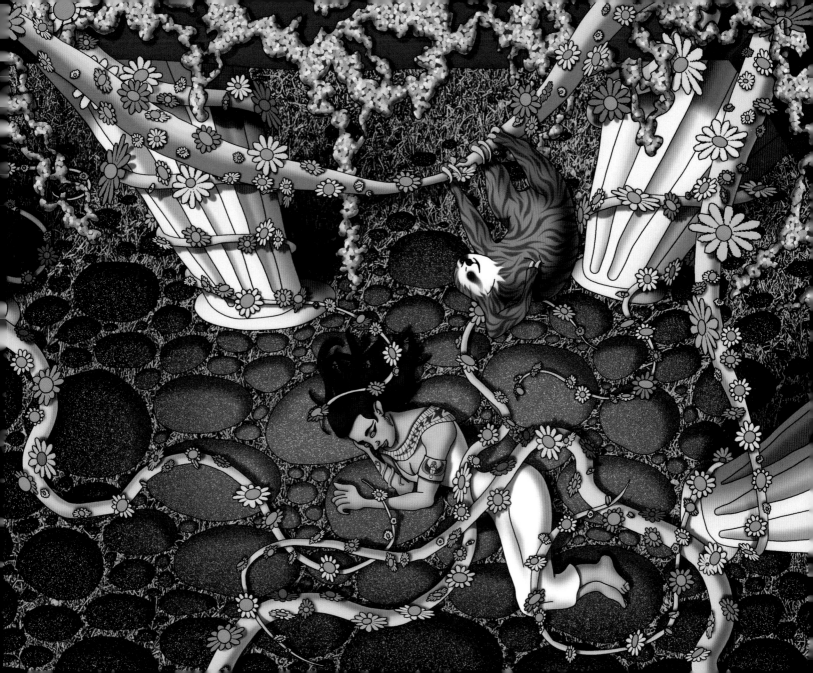

Doctor Price is an eminent expert on spiders.
She led the field at the top of her game.
The only people she loved more than her spiders,
were her baby and husband when she was a dame.

One winter they both got gravely ill.
Scarlet fever had swept through the town.
Eventually, sadly, they both passed away.
Then, mentally, she nearly went all the way down.

Her only solace was her clutter of spiders.
They became her family, and she would not leave the house.
Now, she only has conversations with them,
well...them, and the occasional visiting mouse.

Captain Flint and his squid love sailing the sea.
Whooshing along leaves them feeling free.

They don't care where they're going, as long as it's far.
All they need is the sea, their ship, and a star.

Penelope Jones is a very strange girl,
and she's always been obsessed with bats.
One day, at twilight, she was bitten by one,
while rescuing it from a clowder of cats.

Her wound got infected, so she went to a doctor.
He said "...left untreated you'd surely have died.
Here, take these pills for a week and you'll heal."
One week later, her brain was totally fried.

She became sensitive to light, and temperature too.
So, she and her bat moved to a cave at the zoo.
Now, upside down, they both like to sleep.
They live in their cave and don't make a peep.

When "Doctor" Goodwell inevitably rolls into a town,
hoastfully, he begins luring folks all around.
In fact, he's a conman, a swindler, a thief.
He has quite the knack for changing beliefs.

He begins, "LADIES AND GENTS, please gather around,
and witness my fantabulous Elixir of Life!
MY miracle elixir will shock and astound......
NEVER AGAIN need you find yourselves under a knife!

I discovered it deep in the jungles of Nill,
at the end of a river which flows up a hill.
An obscure tribe at the end of this river partakes of its liquid and NEVER gets ill.

In fact, all it takes is 3 drops on the tongue,
to cure ANY ailment you're suffering from!
This fantastical discovery seems too good to be true,
but believe me, it will do WONDERS for you!"

As "Doctor" Goodwell distracts the folks with his savvy,
his weasel, Shadow, stealthily moves through the crowd......
searching for items of a valuable nature,
and acquiring as much as time would allow.

Mr. Addams and his rat are the closest of friends.

They love binging shows from beginning to end.

In fact, that's pretty much all that they do.

They're also adept at acting them too.

They've both got talent for doing impressions.

They also both suffer from chronic depression.

Rōnin Megasaki really loves water;
possibly, even as much as his koi.
But he's been deathly allergic to water,
ever since he was a small boy.

He can't drink nor touch it or his organs melt down.
The upside being he likely won't drown.

Miho, an architect, designed a home 'round her cat.
She lives there too, but her cat is all that.

She spent nine years planning their purrrfect dream house.
Her cherished cat, Sasha, in effect, is her spouse.